THE POETRY OF MOTHERHOOD
BABY·INSPIRED WISDOM FOR THEIR FIRST YEAR

RACHEL BRUHNKE

Dear Kate—
Best of luck with
all! Congratulations,
you're in for the best
ride of your life :·)
♡ ♡ Rachel

outskirtspress
DENVER, COLORADO

The Poetry of Motherhood
Baby-Inspired Wisdom for Their First Year
All Rights Reserved.
Copyright © 2012 Rachel Bruhnke
v3.0

Outskirts Press, Inc.
http://www.outskirtspress.com

ISBN: 978-1-4327-9240-4

Outskirts Press and the "OP" logo are trademarks belonging to Outskirts Press, Inc.

PRINTED IN THE UNITED STATES OF AMERICA

To my daughter Alma for being my constant inspiration

And to

My grandpa for his love of haiku and for showing me that we all have poetry, and teaching, inside of us.

Foreword

Haiku poems describe daily situations in a way that gives the reader a brand new experience of a well-known situation, an "ah ha" moment about a universal truth.

I had been in the hospital for a few days with my new baby, Alma, and was breastfeeding her when suddenly she let out a little whimper, like a "mew" as she was feeding. It was a sound so vulnerable, so innocent, so *new* to me. I sat there stunned by my love, looking down at this tiny angel who had just wrenched my heart forever…and this poem came to me:

Soft whimpers
Heaven-made to break
Mothers' hearts

The poem was sudden and complete-and it came out of nowhere. I thought, "Wow, a haiku. Cool." I forgot about it for a while, but the poem kept coming back to me so I decided to write it down. I had never written a haiku before, so I thought it was a keeper. Little did I know I had just opened the floodgates of baby-inspired poetry to flow from me, because over the next twelve months I wrote, or rather "channeled", over seventy haikus!

These haikus came to me, almost every one just as they are here, and one after another. I finally had to sleep with a pen and notepad next to me because I would wake up some-times at 3:00 in the morning with two complete haikus in my head and I had to write them down! And the really crazy part is that the day my daughter turned 1-year old, I never wrote another haiku. They just simply stopped coming. The Mozart-madness had ended. Whew!...So I started to write about what they meant.

I feel like these poems were baby-inspired in the larger sense: My baby, your baby, *our* babies inspired these words that came through me. I wanted to share them, and the lessons of first-year motherhood and babyhood that they represent.

I wanted Moms to know that the miracle they are living, exhausting and difficult at times, is felt by us all. Not only are we not *alone*, we are, together with the ferocious love that our babies elicit, a very powerful force. A force to be reckoned with if we harness and direct it.

Since starting this book, our country has begun to experience several crises and the world seems to be ever more tumultuous. For me, that's all the more reason to re-affirm the importance of motherhood, for in that love, that commitment, that *joy*, are the answers. It simply can't be hopeless when we feel what we feel for our babies, all of us, around the world.

We have important work to do, Moms. Our children have a profound and meaningful future to help shape, and we are shaping *now* who they will become in that inevitable future. Let's raise them with love and compassion. The world needs it.

Carl Sandburg, American poet and biographer, has a great quote that "A baby is God's opinion that life should go on." Whatever your religion or not, I think that is right on the mark! While human-devised systems can be questioned, the rock-solidness of our love for our babies is undeniable. Enjoy the poems. Whether wrenching, whimsical or empowering, all our babies wrote them.

A huge thanks and hug to the ladies who helped me get this book out, especially Lynda for her enthusiasm and diligence in reading my draft, and my sister-in-law Karin, who has been cheering me on since both our babies were in strollers together. Paz.

Two sure things:
Breast leakage happens
Spit up, too

Keeping clean as a new mom is definitely not easy. Partially it's a problem of being spit up on, peed and pood on, and of your own leaky breasts. For me, it was about *remembering* that these things were going to happen, several times a day, every day, and taking the necessary precautionary measures.

Either keep a stack of burp cloths where you feed your baby, or just drape them like cobwebs around all the furniture in your house. Put breast pads on *before* you leak! Have tissue or paper towels in the car- always. Bring a bottle of water when you are out, both to drink and to dilute the vomit your baby just deposited on the rug at the public library... Etcetera, etcetera...

They say that insanity is doing the same thing over and over, expecting different results. Blame it on the oxytocin or the lack of sleep, but as a new mom then, I must have been nuts. I was constantly having to re-learn things like, "Oh yeah, my daughter is going to spit up slimy milk on my shoulder, *every time*, after she feeds. How could I have forgotten the burp cloth *again* as I sat down here with her?! Boobs, baby, burp cloth...must remember..."

Another fun one I seemed to forget a lot was that my breasts leaked, and often. How many times was I caught in public, strutting down the isle at the supermarket, say, with two big wet patches on my shirt, signaling to the world, "Not only am I a Mom, but I'm *nuts*, so watch me go!" Ah, the ecstasy (and insanity!) of a proud, new mom...

Morning stares
Limitless questions
In her eyes

Mornings are often good times for babies. They are well rested for the most part, even though *you* may not be, and they have just had a yummy mommy breakfast. Try to make sure you can relax with your baby at this time, on your bed with books and stuffed animals, or just the two of you. Just be together. Before you know it, your infant will be a pre-toddler and *way* too active to sit and coo into your eyes for what seems like hours on end.

These were some of the most captivating times in the early months for me with my daughter. I fell in love with those eyes, and we began to communicate our love through just looking at each other. Consider it building a reserve of unconditional love from which you might be making hefty withdraws in the evening "colicky" (read: *insane*) time of day. You'll once again be gazing into the silent, deep curiosity of those otherworldly eyes.

Soft whimpers
Heaven–made to break
Mothers' hearts

It is no accident that the tiny coos and mews and bird-like chirps of your precious infant send you into the la la land of love. Call it God or biochemistry, the *result* is that our baby's tiny, innocent sounds are meant to take our breath away, and to literally knock us off our feet so that we will stop running around the bush, or the shopping mall, and just *be* with our babies. It's Mother Nature's way of keeping the ever-active woman, now a much-needed mother, firmly planted next to her incredibly vulnerable charge.

In fact, the hormone oxytocin is still surging through your body from pregnancy, and Ecstasy move over! Oxytocin is really the ultimate "love drug". So become addicted to this love drug, because thrill you or scare you, you are *not* baby-sitting. This one's for keeps, so spend your time in awe of your new treasure. Swoon with love, and "waste" your time in wonder as your baby grows and changes. These are transcendent emotions you are feeling now. Harness them and you will know Peace, maybe enough to believe that Peace is Possible for us all.

Baby's mews
Make we mothers muse
On such love

Full moon's glow
Miraculous in
Her dark eyes

Babies love the changes in natural light that happen throughout the day. If you have plenty of windows (or better yet, go outside!), your baby will show you just how fascinating shadows and reflections and dappled light can be. Who knew?

Undoubtedly, you will have many "sessions" of dawn feedings in the early months, possibly followed by a wide-awake infant. Instead of trying to stifle sobs of sleepiness (yours, not hers), take a deep breath, put on the coffee, and hold your baby close while you greet the dawn together. There's no one luckier in the world than you at that moment.

At dusk, especially if your baby is colicky, one of your best remedies can be to *take her outside*! Go for a walk in your neighborhood, step out into your apartment's common area, pace your balcony, whatever "outside" is in your reality. Again, the early evening light and its mysterious shadows may be enough to keep your little werewolf at bay for a bit, and the stroll and change of scenery will relax both of you.

Take advantage, too, of the nighttime light. In just a few months your baby will be sleeping more at night, and depending on the season, may even be going to bed before it is fully dark. So look for the moon those first months, and make sure not to miss it with your baby when it's full and near full. Talk about great shadows! Depending on where you live, too, there may even be enough stars to catch your baby's attention and keep her riveted at the heavens in silent wonder.

All I am
Saying, is please give
Sleep a chance!

Please know something now: Delirium happens. And when it hits, it will be too late (literally) to do anything about it but work through it. So try to get that night routine down ASAP, and do whatever you can to make up for the sleep you will lose in those first weeks and months. Sleep deprivation, like donut-damage, is cumulative. And real. Get your sleep during the day, especially in the first few months, because your baby deserves, and frankly will not settle for anything *less,* than having her needs met in the middle of the night.

So that you don't end up feeling dangerously sorry for yourself when that delirium does strike in the middle of the night, take advantage of her daytime naps. Try to really enjoy them as luxurious, not just the life-savers that they are. Try to pretend that you're *lazing* with your baby when you nap with her in the daytime (who *else* in America gets to do this on a weekday anyway?), and not that you're making up for only having had a total of 4 hours sleep the night before. Ugh.

It is much better to nap with your baby than to spend time reading books about how to get your baby to nap. Just as you are ready to dog-ear that page and close your eyes… her nap will be over! Maddening.

Sleep, per chance
I knew it once, as
In a dream…

Four A.M.
Pat, pat, rub, rub, rub
Please babe, burp!

Four A.M. is *not* the time to learn about burping, so here it goes…If you ever, in your pre-mom life, saw another mom burp her baby and thought she was patting him too hard, you were probably mistaken. Novice burpers don't realize that to get a baby to burp you have to, um, whack 'em a bit. It sounds harsh, but once you've gotten the hang of it you will realize it is true.

Then, when Grandpa tries to burp your baby by tapping just his fingertips on his back and cooing into your baby's ear, you will be the first to roll your eyes, tap your toes, counting the seconds before Gramps shrugs sheepishly, and hands your now crying, still unburped, baby back to you… so that you can give him a good no-nonsense, down-to-business *thump*!

The rule of thumb pretty much is that you should hear it in the same room-but not in the next room. There are three main positions and one *really* good trick that I have found for successful burping:

The first position is the classic, the "missionary position" of burping: With a burp cloth placed (fully!) over one shoulder, place your baby's belly against your chest. Holding him under his darling diapered rump with the palm of one hand, give moderate thumps on his back with the other.

The second position is to sit your baby on your lap facing out. Bend him slightly forward with one hand flat on his chest/stomach area, a burp cloth draped over your hand.

Then pat your baby's middle-upper back with the palm of your other hand. Voilà.

The third position was my mom's favorite, but I never really got the hang of it: Placing your baby on your lap, tummy down, rub and pat your baby's back until she burps. (Don't forget the burp cloth on this one or you'll be changing your pants for sure.)

Lastly, is the *trick*. It works to get your baby's bubbles to the surface, like flicking a medicine dropper with your fingers does: Sitting your baby on your lap after eating, gently bounce your baby up and down a few times before putting him into your tried and true burping position.

She's asleep
But my head spins with
Phantom Cries

Boy, is it hard to come down when you're a new mom! Even when *they're* down, *our* heads still spin. If you're jumping from "phantom cries", those cries you hear in your head when they are actually peacefully asleep, you are not alone!

There are a few remedies. Some moms invest in an audio monitor. That way you can have it by your baby while he sleeps so you won't feel the need to hover over him (yes, I've done it, too!). It allows you to at least get in the other room and close the door, or to go the adjacent condo of your new neighbor-friend (front doors open, of course!) to relax and physically separate for a bit from your nursery-home. Part of seeking out that "Modern Day Village".

Come to think of it, you're baby is down-what are you doing awake anyhow?

Grunts, groans, chirps
My baby, "asleep"
Can she breath?

Whoever came up with the saying "sleeping like a baby" definitely did not HAVE a baby. Sure, when they're out, they're *out*, but those blessed moments can be agonizingly short. Much of the time, many babies seem to be adjusting their bodies, their minds and their vocal chords while they are so-called "asleep". I call it "rockin' and rollin'". Of course, this makes moms *nuts*, but I guess Mother Nature figured that keeping us on our toes in the first months of our babies' lives was way more important than keeping us *sane*! Thanks again, "Mother"!

The best thing you can do while they sleep? Leave the room! The worst thing you can do? Hover over them like I did, worrying if they're choking, shooshing them, trying to adjust their crib so they keep still. It just distracts them from sleep and tunes them into you, the hovering mother, and doesn't allow either one of you to relax. It will also keep you bent over in that back-breaking, not to mention neurotic position potentially even past their first birthday! I bought bears with live heart beats, "lambies", music boxes and ultra-soft organic blankies None of them worked for long, but at the time $25.00 seemed worth even a two-day reprieve, and the illusion of rest.

Try to remember though that especially during naps, which are shorter intervals, some babies "rock and roll"… so just "go with it". Also, as your baby's nighttime sleep regulates, they will sleep for longer periods without needing you, but they still sleep in "cycles", fidgeting a bit in between them. Sleep cycles are about an hour long, and we adults have them, too. Past six or seven months, depending, you can almost time when your baby will "wake up". Just about every hour. Try not to DO anything with them, as of course, yours truly learned too late. The earlier your baby learns to keep sleeping through these cycles the better, for both of you.

Formula,
Buyer beware, can
Dry your milk

If you're not careful, you'll walk out of the hospital with 5 packs of "free sample" formula milk from the ever-generous Nestle Corporation. You'll want to take it because, well, who doesn't grab free samples? But understand, for millions of years babies have been using their mommy's breasts as the nursing bottle, and we're now near 7 billion people on the planet (no comment), so our bodies must have evolved to get the job done, no?

So have faith in your faucets-and keep your baby on them! "Scheduled" feeding, as well as restricting access to your angel kneading at your breasts will reduce your milk flow, so that you'll feel compelled to go to formula. This, of course, means your breasts are given even *more* time off the job, making mother nature think they are not necessary for milk anymore, further reducing your flow. And so on and so on...

It is often hard in the U.S. today to have anything resembling the normalcy of a mother-infant relationship. Most of us must work outside the home, and painfully, many moms must return to that work within just months of giving birth. This of course changes the rules on how we can feed our babies, so we do the best we can to stay natural-and sane-while faced with the nagging sense that this is not OK for our families. When public assistance was more accessible it was easier for new moms to stay home with their infants, like they get to in Europe. Stick together, Moms, things will change. Let's figure out that change together.

Conductor:
Arms flail, head tosses
Her own tune

Sometimes new moms are concerned because their babies' limbs appear, well, *out of control*. Don't worry, they literally *are* out of control, and it's normal. Actually, that startling and flailing around that's tripping you out is called the Moro Reflex. It's an evolutionary hold over from when our ancestors were tree-swingin' fur-grabbers. It helped us hold onto our ancestral mommies while they looked for lunch in the jungles of yore. Cool, huh? Now it's just there of course to give us *one more thing* to worry about as to the health of our child!

Your baby's nervous system is not physiologically quite developed yet and is at the mercy of the Moro Reflex. Imagine, too, all the new stimuli she is exposed to now, and all of it without the constant comfort of your squishy, warm, dark uterus to support her. Poor baby is right!

Actually, that flailing was one of the main reasons I had to swaddle my daughter when she slept. She would be fast asleep and suddenly an arm would flail out, whacking herself in the face, pulling out her pacifier, waking her up, crying. It was like watching a rubber band suddenly pull tight, then slowly shrink back to its normal shape. Weird, Alma. Sometimes it would take one, two, three flails in a row, a head toss back seized with tension for her to then ease into calm. But often that was enough to wake her. Ay! It took my daughter four months to earn her freedom from sleep-swaddling because of those wild arms of hers. Another good reason to keep their nails clipped, too!

Also important to consider if your baby is easily startled: Make sure when breastfeeding to have your hand behind her head or you will run the risk of being painfully, um, *stretched* by a sudden uncontrollable Moro-yank of her head. Ouch!

Obsessed with
who and how she is
Sweet Affair

This is one of my favorite baby-inspired poems! It's exactly what I felt: A love, an obsession, a fascination with my baby. And the cool thing was, like the best affairs, it was mutual. It wasn't going to end in a painful break-up. It wasn't going to end with one of us stopping loving the other, or "finding another", or getting bored in the relationship, or second-guessing it. This was *true love*, forever... Ah, Peace at last....

Even when my baby didn't act like it-being fussy, screaming in my face, rejecting a morsel of food or a toy lovingly given, all while giving *me* the raspberry-I just knew she loved me, too! However, you should know that at first, you aren't going to get any emotional reactions-or interaction-from the love of your life. It's not you, or your baby. It takes a couple of months to start getting responses from your baby that you could call Earthly. Until then, Mom, you're in love with an alien being.

From nowhere
Come floods of joy, fear
Mama's Tears

For some moms it can take a bit, for others it is immediate, but you will love, love, *love* your baby. There is just no other way to describe it. You will be flooded with tenderness, overcome with gratitude for this little creature who at first can barely focus on your face. You will look at him and think, and maybe say-thank you my darling, for saving my life. Thank you for filling me with such joy, such love, such purpose…

Of course, as a teenager he may tell you to "Get a *life*, Mom. Get *another* purpose besides me!" (Ah, isn't irony grand?) Don't worry though. Let it give you a chuckle now. Remember this moment as a new mom when and if that teenage moment comes and right now just call, or channel, your own mother! And thank her.

Grandparents
are still your parents,
Just "smarter"

*All Mothers
understand that the
Earth is round*

As new moms our hormones are going wild-again! They are re-adjusting to regulating just one person, you, as an individual once again. So give yourself a break when the tears come. You have the passion of the oceans inside of you, both hormonal and spiritual, and it is very, *very* real. We all become "bleeding hearts" as new moms, and it's a good thing. Feel the power of knowing that it is not *money* that makes the world go round, but this insane, insatiable torrent of a mother's love.

Allow the love you feel for your baby to fill your heart, and your actions, with oodles of sweet forgiveness and revolutionary compassion. Don't let the naysayers and the warmongers confuse your new mother's heart. Being a mother can turn you into at once a forgiving, life-affirming soul, but also a tigress against all things violent.

Understand, have in your conscious mind as you take your baby to the breast with such love and devotion, that so too are hundreds of millions of women around the world. What would you wish for them and for their babies? Remember that. Imagine that. It's called solidarity, and it will help you raise your baby with peace and with power, and will help your child also to find his or her *purpose*.

If we can honor and trust that tigress-mother, see it in one another's eyes and *act* on it, we just might save the world…Aren't babies powerful!?

Enamored
of my baby's Doc
Grateful Mom

You will *love* you baby's pediatrician. In fact, depending on the your marital and/or mental state, you may even think you have a crush on him, so happy are you that this person knows and cares for your baby; not like you do of course, but in some ways *better*. Your baby's doctor, for example, can diagnose and cure an ear infection, when the best you could figure out from your baby's crying was that it was a "growth spurt" and she needed to eat more.

Watching that doctor hold your baby, turn her over, check her little body may warm you to tears. It almost always did me. Alma's doctor must have thought I was a real nut. I'd get weepy-eyed every time he took out his stethoscope, loving how he was helping my baby!

Don't be self-conscious, though. Pediatricians by their own admission are a "special" kind of doctor. They understand that you have the "love hormone" oxytocin coursing through your body. They appreciate it because remember, the heart-wrenching fact is that *they* love your baby, too. That's why they chose their profession. So, a shout out to pediatricians!

…Now, if we can only get a health care system in this country that will give us enough of these lovely doctors so that they aren't so busy and can spend a few more moments with each of their patients, and their nuts-o moms.

Diaper leaks
Anathema to
Peaceful sleep

Imagine the scenario: You've come to the end of the last "round" of the day with your baby of Feed, Burp and Change. You-and your baby-are exhausted. Swaddled tight, she's (stiff) putty in your arms. Her eyes are closed, her breathing regular. Finally. You creep silently toward the bed, a sigh of exhaustion and relief welling up inside of you. As you lay her down, caressing her body one last, soothing time, you feel it-a wet spot on her side! No God, please, no! She has peed, and the diaper you just changed (before you finally got her to sleep in your arms) has leaked! Against hope you lay her down anyway, thinking to your delirious now tearful self that, "maybe she won't notice". You lay down next to her, ever so slowly your head touches the pillow…and she begins to squirm.

It is agonizing to be so exhausted you could cry. It can be maddening to have just gotten your baby to *stop* crying, to then have all your (in) tense efforts go to waste on a leaky diaper. Make sure to take the precaution to put your baby's diaper on evenly. The squirming sleep only gets worse as the months pass, and for some reason they become allergic to being on their backs. So get in the habit early of getting that diaper symmetrical on that little body!

Also, especially in the early months when first teaching your baby to fall asleep (did you even *know* you had to do that before becoming a mom?), it's a good habit to make a fresh diaper a requisite of putting her down. No matter what. Your sanity is worth 25 cents, or another clean cloth.

But know that try as you might to make everything perfect, plan the routine, "set the stage" for sleep, you just never know what is going to happen. Ay! Just *breathe* when it does…!

> *After hours*
> *of night care-taking*
> *A dog barks*

Your newborn
Toughest job you'll
ever miss

People always say about a baby's first year, "The time passes so fast", or "It's over before you know it". Yes, there is the inevitable feeling that time speeds up when we have kids, but the reality is, time *isn't* going faster, we are.

While much of this is inevitable because of our responsibilities, we can also consciously choose to slow down. Remember the lazy days of summer as a kid? Now is your time, with your infant, to bask in the imposed mellowness they can make you feel-if you let it. The irony is that it is our race *against* time that actually gives us the impression of time speeding up. It is when we slow *down* that days and hours get longer.

There is a lot to complain about and feel overwhelmed by when you are taking care of your beloved newborn. When you feel this way, try to take a breath, and remember that this is the most meaningful, lovely work you will ever do. Adapt to your baby's rhythm, not that of corporate America. Time is *not* money, thank you very much. Time is *free*, and precious, and luxurious. Learn from your baby and soak it up…had a nap lately? Paradoxically, the day will actually slow down if you take one.

Just try not to do everything at once, or you will find yourself, literally, in absurd positions. What a sight we moms must be at times!

Theater
of the absurd: Mom,
Acrobat

Don't expect
Quick turnarounds at
Night feedings

If you're lucky night feedings will last about 6 months, with the first few months being several times a night. Each "round" (wake, feed, burp, maybe change a diaper, put back to sleep) can take between 20 minutes, if all goes well….to two *hours* if something is wrong, or if you royally screw up.

One time your little angel will wake with a slight coo, suckle softly, burp immediately and slide back quietly into peaceful slumber. A delight! Another night, or the next "round", however, she might get gas cramps, go poop yet you will have forgotten to check her diaper, choke on her milk for some reason and totally wake herself up by gagging… you just never know.

Be prepared for the fluctuation of time or you can get incredibly frustrated and desperate. Not good when it's 3:00 AM, your baby is now crying in your ear, and there's no way *out* of it but to get *through* it, and to solve whatever the problem is…but of course you don't *know* the problem because she can't tell you, so you have to guess, but you might get it wrong, causing her to *scream louder*!…and so on and so on…

An amazing thing happens, however. I remember one of these delightful night horror sessions. Alma screamed and screamed. I had finally figured out what she needed, dealt with it, and put her now quiet, calm little body in my arms. With her screams still ringing in my ears, without thinking I leaned closer toward her and with a universe of tenderness, kissed her forehead. Can you imagine someone 'treating you" as horribly as a baby can, and you forgetting it in an instant afterward? Awesome. Babies are *sure* lucky they feel so precious.

If your baby is a great night sleeper, don't rub it in to others, pleazzzzz! The patience of even the best of friends or closest family will be worn thin by gleeful, bright-eyed (read: well-rested) boasts of having gotten 8 hours, even with a newborn. There is nothing like having night after night interrupted several times by a baby's needs-needs that simply *cannot* be ignored. But I remember my sister, who had older kids, kept telling me, "It gets better. It ends. They sleep." Ah, and when it does happen, the joy you feel will be epic.

> *At four months*
> *The Great Seas parted*
> *and you slept*

Massage is
Worth a thousand words
So do both

With babies, less in not more. So talk, massage, dance and sing with your baby- a lot. Heck, my daughter, crayon placed in her hand did what I called, her first "art piece" at 2 1/2 months! Why not call it that? Silly? Who cares? Crazy? …Don't get me started on what's *really* crazy in this world…

Your baby will love to interact with you, and even before she can show it, is absorbing and thriving on your input. No one has to tell you to "talk to your baby". That comes naturally. Just know that it's good-for both of you. She will be fascinated and comforted by your words and your tone, and you will feel like the best and happiest mommy in the world as you rattle on, sensically or not, to your baby.

As you babble on with silly, spontaneous rhymes to your baby, or gesture and pontificate on the meaning of life to her, people around you will simply marvel. You will probably never be this un-self conscious again in your life (i.e., you won't be babbling and whipping out your boobs everywhere in public) as you discover perhaps for the first time how liberating it is not to *care* what others think! So babbling to your baby is good, and remember, moms have been doing so since the Neanderthals invented talking.

What's cuter?
coos, wiggles or smiles
…Decisions

At about six weeks your baby will wake up. If it's been hard-going before that, take heart because it *will* happen. I remember being nervous because my daughter was colicky in her first month, that I was going to have a grumpy baby, toddler, child, teenager…Ahhh!!! Was it *my* genes or her father's? Who's to blame? Does she love me? Will she ever smile? I just *knew* my family was re-running the family joke about me being a demanding and defensive youngster. Was my daughter going to be some kind of karmic payback?

Breathe…Those first six weeks or so can be interminably long and so full of fears, both expressed and secret. They can also bring up a lot of your "issues" that you thought would miraculously disappear when you gave birth to a new generation of *you*. Try not to worry, and give yourself a break. Most of us go through that. And remember, it's only partly reality, as your hormones are readjusting to being just one person again-a new and better and more whole-you. And alas, like the pain of childbirth, the stinging uncertainty of those first weeks will quickly fade once you see your child's first smile.

Fortunately, it will only get harder to conjure up those earlier frightening emotions when those smiles keep *coming*, when you can even see a sense of humor in her as she reacts with delight to the silly faces you make at her. And she'll wiggle and kick, and pretty soon start her "baby talking", or "cooing".

It's also at this time, at two to three months, that she'll

be more able to "self-entertain", as they call it. She'll find her hands, and her hands will find her mouth, and she can spend a surprising amount of time cooing and chewing in a swing or infant seat.

Of course you'll love to be with her at this time, but it will be so nice to have a break, too; being near her, but with you both contentedly "doing your thing". This is a good time to have other kids around, too. If you invite your little neighbors over, both your baby and they can play together and it's great socialization-for all involved. Little kids love babies and will talk to them and find fun ways to interact. Your baby will be delighted!

Exercise
As they say, does a
Baby good!

When babies are born, they have been crunched up for months in your uterus. They need to stretch! Helping your baby stretch his limbs, his legs, his arms, is great exercise for the first few months. Later, he'll want to stand up and bounce non-stop while you hold him, building up his leg muscles and flexibility. Give him plenty of tummy time on a clean blanket on the floor, with his favorite rattle and soft animals around him. He'll love doing his baby push-ups on them (until he doesn't of course, in which case, distract him *fast*, or you'll get an earful…)

When he has enough upper body strength to push up strongly, put a few toys slightly but not frustratingly out of his reach so he works a bit to get them. You are teaching him to crawl, Mommy! Pretty soon, he'll scoot his knees up under his body (you can help him, too). He'll push up his body with his arms, and voilà, crawling…

Momma exercise is important, too. Yikes, for some of us more than others. Get that bod back in shape, woman! You'll be so much happier when you look back on your baby's first-year pictures if you're looking at how cute *he* was, and not wincing at how enormous *you* still were. What's totally unfair about this mommy exercise thing, though, is that you are exhausted from your non-stop emotional and physical marathon even without exercise, and you may still not be losing the weight! Baby-rearing is not necessarily calorie-burning, so we moms need to take those extra steps, literally. Sling on that baby front pack and get walking!

Exercise will get you back in shape, calm your nerves, and give you a much-needed reality check. Oh yeah, there's the *rest* of the world out here. How did I forget them? You'll gain perspective on your life and your daily, now radically different, routine. Those were some of the most empowering and enjoyable times for me as a new mommy. I was taking care of myself, while providing a calming bonding time with my angel.

We were creating community, too. We were meeting people, learning the nooks and crannies of our neighborhood, being a happy and healthy presence in our surroundings… Mommies and babies making world peace, one-block-at-a-time. Lucky us!

Life is now
spent in 10- minute
Increments

That is to say, only plan for something you can do in ten minutes, which however difficult to imagine, will be pretty much your max "free time" for about a year. Talk about a weight loss plan!

Here are 10 things you can do in 10 baby-free minutes:

1) Collect all the burp rags, blankets, washcloths and baby clothes you've strewn around the house since yesterday (when did you get so *messy?*)
2) Clean spit up stain on couch (Using baby's dirty burp cloth for this task defeats the purpose. Try to get it together enough to get out a clean rag.)
3) Put last night's dishes in the sink to soak. Mutter about wasteful people and their dishwashers. Wish you had a dishwasher. Chastise yourself for that thought.
4) Write half an email to your girlfriend with two kids. "…I had no *idea* what you went through until now...!" Follow your new grammar rule of using zero punctuation. Smile because you know your friend will understand, as you now understand her. Give a shout out for solidarity mamas around the world. Cry quickly for mamas in the world…Vow to have sex *soon*, so you will stop being so nuts!
5) Sort laundry into baby and mommy clothes. Throw into washer mixed up anyway.
6) Fold 1/3 of the laundry when done. (If you do the math here, "doing laundry" can take 3 days. Alas.)
7) Take a piece of bread out of the bag (discard the

twist tie as a waste of time). Tear off a piece of lettuce (decide washing is a waste of time) and cut a slice of value brand mega-cheese. Fold ingredients together. Shovel into mouth while standing over sinkful of dirty dishes (worry that you are teaching your baby horrible table manners).

8) Read a page of your "First Year Baby Guide Book". As you read about how her poop will change over the next months, dream of your baby and cry at how much you love her…Vow to have sex *soon*, so you will stop being so nuts!

9) Change the plastic tub on your Diaper Genie. Say a quick Earth Prayer for all the resources you are using to take care of your baby in America. Feel better that at least you've saved a bit of water by not having showered in 3 days.

10) Decide that 3 days is too long not to shower and jump in. Take a deep luxurious breath while you start to shampoo. Wonder if you just heard your baby cry…

While we're at it, here are 10 things you can do in 10 seconds, too:

1) Press "send" on that half-written email to your veteran mommy friend. Don't bother finishing, she'll understand.

2) Fill your 10th glass of water for the day. (Wonder, "Does breastfeeding really make me this thirsty or am I just paranoid about my milk production?")

3) Panic about your milk production.

4) Nuke that cup of coffee you have yet to get to this morning. (Find it still there at noon when you go to warm up your baby's mashed carrots. No *wonder*

you've been on the verge of passing out all day!)

5) Check in on your sleeping baby to see if she's still breathing.

6) Read the Baby Blues comic strip. Laugh out loud.

7) Check out your rear end in the mirror, or worse yet, your stomach.

8) Check out your breastfeeding cleavage in the mirror to (sort of) make up for # 7.

9) Sniff your nursing bra to see if it'll stand one more day without washing. Do this for two more days.

10) Look at the clock and calculate…everything!

Her closed eyes:
Crescent Moons shooting
Black sun rays

Boy, when you look at your baby's sleeping face, the poetry will positively pour from your heart! Part of that is love and part, of course, are the endorphins (nature's blessed morphine) your body releases once you have finally gotten her to sleep. Take those moments to study her precious face before you put her oh-so-carefully down.

Use the occasion for a replenishing moment of calm and peace with your baby. Careful though, you'll be tempted to kiss and squeeze her scrumptious sleeping self all over, and into wakefulness. Ay, the Gods must be crazy to tease a mother like that!

But instead of doing something nuts-o like waking your precious sleeping baby, put her down, and find a permanent place for that love-gush. Draw her face, paint a quick impression of your feelings, write her a love letter, or heck, a poem.

You don't have to be an artist or a writer to put your love on paper. Somehow, even if it's just once, or a few times while she's a baby, do something permanent. Make sure to keep those scraps of paper in the baby book "to do" box. You will get to it eventually, and she will have it forever.

Morning bed
full of smiles and laughs
Sacred Space

Parents are all over the map on whether or not to share the bed with their babies. Whatever you decide, when making that choice, just keep in mind that probably the vast majority of humanity shares a bed with their infants. It is a combination of necessity and culture no doubt, but that proximity nurtures a life-long interdependence that helps keep kids and parents, i.e. families, bound together. Don't feel strange or needy if your choice is to have your baby sleep with you!

On the other hand, many American parents don't want to encourage that life-long mutuality (i.e., still living at home at 30!). They see their responsibility as raising their children to be independent, not interdependent. It's an individual choice. Whether you decide to "co-sleep" or not, morning "bedtime" with your baby is a cozy, relaxing and loving way to start the day.

Children are
the ties that bind both
You and Me

I don't know about you, but while I was raising Alma in her first year, it was like babies-and mommies-were coming out of the woodwork. Where had all these children and baby-related things *been* before? Not to mention the support of other mothers. Suddenly, a once cut and dry transaction with the grocery store cashier turns into a mommy solidarity session, shared photos and all. A mishap at the mall and moms are there with a helping hand and an extra diaper wipe. Wow! The corporate world has nothing on "networking" moms.

It got me thinking about the anti-war song by Sting in the 80's about him hoping that the Russians loved their children too. Children connect us. They are not only "the future", a line that unfortunately has become an empty cliché. Children are the present, the *ultimate* here and now. Just ask a mom. We should be living in a world, in societies, whose very function is to help make families function. If not, what are we all doing?

Children tie all of us together. It is what all of us around the world have most in common. Not only do I know that the Russians love-and always *did* love-their children, but Arabs love their children believe it or not, and Americans from both Blue states and Red states, too. Some day, the powers that be will reflect this reality. Raise your children to help make it happen and you will have done right by them, and by us all.

For babies
Happiness is in
Your timing

I'm embarrassed to say, but I feel like it took me weeks to realize that, oh yeah, *I* need to put my baby to sleep; *she* can't do it on her own! For the first three months of your baby's life, she is all about getting her sleeping and eating skills regulated, and that is a monumental task. She needs your help, your guidance. Think of her as a tiny boat on a sometimes wild sea. The energy of that sea is her physical needs and her fright at the newness of it all. You, her Mother, are the water, the ocean of comfort that nestles her in that wild energy.

Get your timing and her signals right, and things will go more smoothly. Learn her signs for sleepy, for example, and you will avoid a lot of tears-from both of you. For the first couple of months, not much is going on with your little alien, except eat, wake, sleep…eat, wake, sleep…Try not to overstimulate her, or the tears (and screams!) will come.

After a couple of months when your baby "wakes up" however, the timing will change. Your breasts will often not lull your little charge into sleepy la la land. More often, they will stimulate her to be awake, and stare, and coo, and smile-and play. And here's the cruel irony: There is something about breastfeeding that is so mellowing for mommy…and combined with massive sleep deprivation, you'll just want to…doze…Bad timing, Mommy! Because your baby will now be energized, not mellowed, by a belly full of warm milk. Get ready to play-and don't even *think* about trying to talk her out of it, because guess who's going to win? Just *try* to put her down when she really just wants to be awake. Watch out!

Breastfeeding
With hands idle can
Spell trouble

It doesn't matter how enamored you are with the idea of breastfeeding, or what wonderful, modern fathers and grandfathers say about it. The *reality* of breastfeeding is it can be very tedious. Don't feel bad when you feel that way. If it is hard for you to slow down once you *sit* down to feed your baby, you are not alone. When your mind is spinning from all that you need to do, having to sit idle for 20 minutes every couple of hours can be maddening. Of course we are lucky to be moms, thank you very much, and it is amazing and empowering and tigress and all that…but at times it can be outright *boring*.

There are many things to do that are constructive, yet relaxing while you're stuck in that comfy chair with your angel on your breast. You can snack on something healthy, imagining that what goes in your mouth goes through your breast and into your baby's mouth. Take this time to read (or to write a poem!), draw your angel's face, cut (not bite!) your nails, make a mellow social call, something that will relax and delight you. Learn to meditate and breathe; use these times to practice. It's a skill you'll need for the crazy toddler years, the busy school years and the yo-yo teenage years, so you might as well learn it now while you are *forced* to sit!

And of course, make sure you and your baby are comfortable. A super invention is the "boppy", a half donut-shaped, firm, wrap-around pillow. Your baby lays couched sideways on it while she feeds, and you can rest your arms high up on it, too, to hold her comfortably. It also seconds as a comfy "couch" that semi-sits your baby up before she can on her own, so you can get your hands free while she coos with a rattle or something. Or turn her on her tummy on it, and she'll start learning to push up against it.

Another great investment, and I still have it today, is a slanted footstool. When your feet are on it, it helps to perfectly balance the weight of you and your baby while you are sitting, and is a great back saver. Worth it!

Comfortable, cozy, closer to your baby than you'll ever be…Breastfeeding, over all, is magical.

Three a.m.
baby, breast and me
Silent World

"Have Done" lists
are as needed as
"To Do" lists

Hey, Moms! I have an idea: As much as we remind ourselves of the things that remain to be done today, let's recognize the things we have *already* done today, too. Don't get me wrong. I am a super fan of "To Do" lists. I couldn't make it in adulthood without them. (Come to think about it, as "get pregnant" was #1 on my "To Do" list since my early 30's, I might not be a mom without them, either.)

However, this is not an "either/or", but rather a "both/and" situation. Here's how you can do it:

1) Take a moment in the early afternoon when your baby is busy self-entertaining.
2) SIT DOWN for Heaven's sake!
3) Take a breath and think to yourself, "What have I done today already by (*insert time*) P.M.?"

You will be amazed at all the things you actually accomplish most days, both baby and non-baby related, while you thought you were just lost in the haze of it all. (Note, Moms: Make this list as a mental, not a written, exercise that takes just a moment. If not, you run the risk of creating another task "To Do", Heaven forbid.)

Ok, this is what I am talking about. Here's what I came up with by 1:30 P.M. the day Alma inspired me to write this poem. It made me smile:

1) Got myself and my daughter dressed and fed, and the bed semi-made.

2) Took care of both her and her cousin (two 9-month-olds!) in a 4-hour time swap with my brother.
3) Showed both babies how to stop and smell roses while on our morning stroll. Literally.
4) Had an e-mail exchange that resulted in securing medical coverage for my daughter and me.
5) Called my mom.
6) Found a groovy new way to keep my daughter self-entertained for 10 minutes straight (a box filled with clothing that she can take out, toss around and play in).
7) Did 15-minutes of floor exercises while playing with the kids on the ground in the living room.
8) Remembered to SIT DOWN, once, which resulted in this poem…

Predict the
Unpredictability
of babies

Wow, babies are a lesson in flexibility and patience. One day they're great sleepers, the next day you can't seem to get them down. They say that we "learn" so much from our children. With babies, I think observation is one of the biggest lessons that we learn.

Babies are curative in today's overly busy world. They force us to slow down and to observe. In order to know them and what they need, *we* need to be in tune, both with them and with ourselves.

When people say that baby's are hard work, I think the hardest thing is figuring out why they're crying! The books will say, "Feed when hungry", "Put down to sleep when tired". Huh? Which cries are those, the shrieking wail, the pitiful whimper, the hearty protest cry? I'm not a penguin. I can't tell my baby's cry among a brood of a thousand others! My senses are not *that* tuned.

Babies will cry from overtiredness, so if he's tired but you think he's hungry and try to feed him, he'll go crazy... Babies will cry from hunger, so if you think he's tired and try to put him down hungry, ay! What's a momma to do?... Except trust her senses, and relax into imperfection.

A baby's needs
Not hard to meet but
Hard to know

Admitting
I'm tired of her
I shudder

No matter how nuts-o you are for your new baby, they are positively exhausting and you *will* get tired of the work of it sometimes. You can't think they're cute 24/7, no matter how insanely in love you are. Sometimes, when you are tired or bored or freaked out enough about whatever, your baby's coos will be positively ba humbug! Forgive yourself, it doesn't mean anything. It's still true love.

It's vital to forgive yourself when this happens. It is completely natural and inevitable. And this, too, shall pass. You're doing great. Remember, our bodies, minds and souls have had a million years of practice at caring for our infants. You are an *expert* inside, and we are the ones chosen for this task. Lucky us!

Feed, change, rock
God, is there relief?
…Let's hope not

Tiny toes
While other end feeds
Flex and curl

Ah, those tiny, chubby, wrinkly feet! It's fascinating to watch them move, flexing and curling away, toes constantly kneading the air as she suckles steadily at her other end. Babies' feet are a delight!

Like many other early mementos, I kept my daughter's footprint from the hospital. It's at the beginning of her 1-year scrapbook. In there, too, is a picture entitled "first pair of shoes". Those are the ones your baby will wear for 20 seconds, and then kick off screaming in protest. Save money on the shoes, don't even buy them! Socks with rubber pads to keep them from slipping when you "practice walk" with her are fine, and they even make darling ones now that look just like shoes.

It's best, too, to keep your baby barefoot as much as possible. The bottoms of our feet are ticklish, so babies will tend to curl them up a bit as they practice walking. This will help them develop more curved arches on the soles of their feet for their whole lives. So, off with the shoes!

Keep his feet clean, though! Babies will discover their fascinating lil' appendages around 4 or 5 months, and they won't be able to keep their hands-or mouths-away from them. Unlike fingernails, though, you won't have to clip his toenails for a while, pretty much until you see the first scratch on your baby's tender leg. Then by all means, clip away, and of course beat yourself up for neglect of your precious charge because he scraped himself....Ugh.

Silly grins
eyes flutter, half shut–
Baby Dreams

It is quite possible that the first smile you see from your baby will be while he is sleeping. Babies are fascinating to watch in their REM sleep. Their fluttering and twitching remind me of how you see dogs and cats dream sometimes, paws racing, mouth snarling and twitching…Babies do a similar thing, but one wonders, "What can she *possibly* be dreaming about? She's 11 weeks old!" Then comes the lovely thought: She's probably dreaming of *you*, since you are most of her world. Wow, thanks baby! You're dreamy, too.

So watch her dreaming for a bit, make a record of it somehow so you will never forget it…and then take a nap! It doesn't matter if the house is a disaster, your food's backed up so you had to serve cheerios as a meal. Hey, it's a *grain*, all right? (Ten lashes tonight when you can't sleep because of worry and guilt.) Both of you *must* nap, or beware the rest of the day…

Morning naps
If not taken will
leave their mark

Evening howls
of dreaded colic
Cause unknown

I still remember the CD I used to use to calm Alma down in her early evening colic sessions. It was the Cuban artist Silvio Rodriquez, well known for his ballads of strong love and struggle. I used to hold her in my arms and sing and dance to the righteous, beautiful songs. I think she felt my passion for the music, and that is what would eventually calm her.

Whatever it is, try asking a mom whose child had colic "what it was like", and you will get the same response: First, a respectful pause and deep breath as the nightmarish images of their inconsolable infant flood back from memory. Then, the stories...True, one tends to embellish with time a bit, as men do with fishing stories, that their baby "cried for 5 hours every night for 3 months", etc...It just seems like it was that long, but however long it actually *was*, it made up for it in intensity. Colic is an *intense* experience.

My daughter was "colicky" for 6 weeks, 2 hours every early evening. So, 6 weeks is 42 evenings x 2 hours = 84 hours of crazy, inconsolable, did-I-mention *loud* crying. It's an indelible and nerve-frazzling experience, but if you are experiencing it currently, know: Colic *does* end.

There are two defenses against dreaded colic: soothe your baby or distract her, totally. I would put Alma in the baby front pack and head out the front door! Walking and talking nonsense and pointing at everything, just to keep her off the witching hour.

"Fussy babies", colicky or not, can greatly benefit from "swaddling". There is a great book, <u>The Best Baby on the Block</u> that talks about this, and helped me understand how vulnerable babies feel. The comfort of swaddling greatly helped my daughter, and me, through those first scary, insecure months.

Swaddled tight
She's my little grub
So calm now

Razor nails
Rake innocent breast
Clippers, please!

The calcium that your baby is sucking up all day long, besides making her body bigger, is also making her nails grow like crazy! And who knew that her excruciatingly delicate little fingers could produce absolute calcium-rich weapons at the tips! My daughter did actually draw blood once while I was breastfeeding her.

I called it even though, because I remember the first time I clipped those nails of hers, trying to be so careful, I actually cut her a wee bit and drew *her* blood! Note to you novice Moms: If you inadvertently slightly injure your infant, *never* tell her about it later-she will never forget it. My daughter has said to me as a pre-schooler, "Remember when I was a baby, Mom, and you were cutting my nails and made me bleed?" Ugh, child. Honestly!

So, here's the best way to clip that I've heard from many moms, and it worked for us. It's one-two-three: Once from each side, clip clip, then the tip in the middle. Clip. You don't have much time because babies often do not like getting their nails clipped, so coo and chatter to your baby to distract her. Or you can try it when she's sleeping, too.

Be disciplined about cutting her nails. Because as baby nails are razor sharp, she can also poke her eyes or even her ears and draw blood. So if you see a spot of blood in her ears, this is probably why. Time for a baby manicure, Mommy!

Night Meter
A digital clock
in the dark

I would have thought that having a baby would have freed me a bit from the regiments of strict timekeeping. Not so, especially at night, when every minute of sleep counts and every nuance of how the night "will go" is reflected-literally and figuratively-in the piercing glare of your digital clock. You place it strategically on your nightstand to be seen immediately-with just one eye open-when you hear your baby cry, or move, or cough in the night.

Take heart. Moms and Dads around the electrified world must be going through the same nightly neon watch:

11:59 PM (A single cry or movement) "Oh no! This is too early for him to be hungry. Do I just put his pacifier back in, or do I feed him and risk him waking up again in a few hours...?"

2:37 AM (Soft cries getting louder) "Ok, this is the middle of the night. I'll just feed him and he'll sleep until 6:00. All is well, don't freak..."

4:03 AM (A whimper) "Ahhh!!! Again?...Not *two* times in one night, *please*!!!!"

You'll wonder how you ever got through the night before without waking up to those red or green digital eyes, staring at you, challenging you to calculate your reality... every two hours, all night long...

It takes a
Modern day village
Seek it out

As American moms, we often try to do too much our-
selves, even while taking care of a newborn. We want to
prove to ourselves and to the world that we can juggle all the
balls at once, successfully and even with aplomb, a la "Look
Ma, no hands!" It's ok. It's what makes us an AmeriCAN
type of people-a people, however, who also had to invent
Prozac for their own use. Resist the temptation therefore
to raise your child *too* much within this "can-do" world of
isolation.

The nuclear family is just that: the nucleus, the *hub*; but
there is also the rest of the cell too, the "extended family". Not
just yours either, but all of the community around you. Know
your neighbors? Been to your local farmers market? Chatted
with the mailman? As a new mom, all of these human re-
sources will seem to be much more important to you-and
much more prevalent! Like, hey! Where did all these baby-
loving people *come* from all of the sudden? Where were all
these mommies and babies and friendly people a year ago?
Cool…

Children have always been raised by a variety of adult
influences. It is eventually what will allow them to interact
well with society, and to feel safe within it. From the first
glowing smiles your pregnant belly may have gotten from
complete strangers on the street, to the coos at your new-
born from the supermarket checker, people *want* to interact
with you and your baby. So let them. We primates are inter-
ested in each other!

Community will come out of the woodwork for you and your baby so enjoy, enrich and entrench those new attachments. Everyone will win if you do: You, your baby, those you bring into your nuclear circle…and remember, when it comes to your own family, try not to hover too much! Let *them* be with your baby, too….

Common ere:
Micromanagement
Spouse, beware!

Transition
Me, she says with screams
softly, please

I had to learn this lesson over and over again, that "transitions" need to be pre-meditated. In our busy world and life, we adults race from one thing to another. Babies simply cannot handle that, and boy will they let you know it-loudly!

Some delicate (i.e., one wrong move and you have a screaming baby on your hands) transitions are: Getting in and out of the car seat, getting in and out of the bath, and diaper changes. Our tendency may be to hold our breath in fear (Please angel, just don't *scream* at me!) and rush through the transition. Wrong move!

One of the most important transition helpers is your calm, soothing voice. Let her know, even by your tone, that she is moving on to the next interesting, and safe, thing. A bath, a diaper change, a care seat, Yeah!

We often clam up when we are approaching tension- and as you are probably finding out, a baby screaming in your face can be in-*tense*. But the last thing you both need if for you to clam up. So take a deep breath before you place her in that car seat. Coo to her, smile, chatter away in a sing-song voice as you hand her a squishy rattle while you slyly clip her in. Distraction is the name of the game.

It exists!
Her "panacea":
Sacred Swing

Get a swing. Yeah, I know, "No child of mine is going to…"; "Gasp! He'll be in my loving arms all the…", "How dare you suggest that I…". I made these exact protestations whenever well-meaning people had the temerity to suggest I get one of the mechanical you-must-not-love-your-baby-gismos. I would mutter to myself about their consumerist, wasteful ways…But yes, Mom: Get a swing if you need it. Especially if you have a so-called "fussy baby", you really will need to find any way you can to get your arms free once in a while. And believe it or not, swings work!

Don't think of it as you neglecting your baby, handing him over to a cold, loveless mechanical device. Your baby will *enjoy* the swing. It will calm him, relax him…and give you time to calm and relax yourself, too. Why do you think hammocks were probably invented? Swings are just modern versions of hammocks (and if you can hang one of those in your house or backyard, great!)

I found that the full-sized swings work the best. But re-member, you don't have to buy it new. Reduce, *reuse*, recycle… Bouncies are good, too, but both will work. Moms, unless you live in a commune, or a very extended family with lots of kids and adults literally an arms-length away, we *need* these things.

Investing in a bouncy, a swing, or a hammock is love and play for your baby, not abandonment! Trust me, when your baby is no longer enjoying the ride, he'll let you know. Soon, your baby's needs will outgrow a swing, and another "panacea" will need to be found. Alas.

Watchful eyes
Following my fork
Make me smile

Ah, solid food! Moms can have so much angst about "when" to start 'em on solids. I prefer the parenting advice in Finding Nemo, when Marlin asks Crush how you know when kids are ready for something. Crush replies, "You don't. But when *they* know, *you'll* know", i.e., they will give you signs. My daughter literally started to *watch* me eat, with a mixture of curiosity and self-pity. "Where's mine, Mommy?" her intense eyes would implore me.

If I had it to do over, I would rather have introduced rice cereal earlier than 4 months, than to have supplemented breastfeeding with formula, only to then lose my own milk. Bummer. The best rule of thumb: Look for those signs that your baby wants to venture into solids. When they know, you'll know. You know?

Try as much as possible to cook her own food. Starting her young life on ready-made baby food just gets you both into a cycle of processed, grab-a-snack, fast food. Yes, I had my daughter on the rice mixture in her first weeks of "solids", but as far as the vegetables and protein, I surprised myself and did them all!

You can also try to get as much produce as you can from the local farmers market. Then you'll know that her food was grown much closer to home than what you get at a supermarket chain. That way you're supporting your local economy, too-the community your baby is growing up in...

Here is a list and simple recipes that Alma gummed her

way through beginning at 4 months to the end of her first year:

Vegetables and fruit:
- Sweet potatoes (try putting in some squeezed orange juice)
- Carrots (with a dash of cinnamon)

These were two of Alma's favorites. Her staples. I cooked them, and mashed them in the blender, then added a *tad* of the "extras", just for flavor. Also good combinations, prepared in the same way, were:

- Squash with olive oil
- Broccoli and zucchini with Parmesan cheese
- Spinach with cream
- String beans with butter
- Sweet baby peas
- Cooked and mashed bananas
- Applesauce (It's way easier to leave the skin on while cooking, then just scoop around it as you feed your baby)

Protein:
- Cottage cheese (still one of her favorites!)
- Morsels of tofu, chicken, turkey or meat mixed in with her other food
- Eggs (with a touch of salt)

All of these (except the eggs and cottage cheese) can be frozen. Fill ice cube trays with the cooked and blended food, and freeze. Take them out of the trays, put them in plastic bags and label. When it's time for your baby to eat, just take out one or two, throw them in the microwave, and presto!

Baby gourmet!

It's a bit of work up front, but these frozen blocks of homemade baby food can last you a week or two. Plus, you'll know your baby was truly fed by *you*. Soon you'll be handing your baby her own spoon, and ah, the delight when she can tackle a snack, and then her own meals, mostly on her own...

Self-feeding
Is akin to mom's
Quiet Time

Night Babble
Worse than hunger, is
playfulness!

Sometimes babies will want to play at the most inopportune times! A case in point: the middle of the night when he's woken up from one of his sleep cycles and you, delirious, have fed and changed him and are ready to pass out again. After all, it's 3:00 AM and you have your rights, right?...Wrong!

You usually know when one of these sessions of Night Babble is going to happen. Your baby will start giggling while you change him, smacking and grabbing your hands, kicking his feet. Meanwhile, you are trying to cope with the reality of what this might mean (Oh God, no! Not now angel, I'm going to pass out!).

You coo lullabies to him, pretending your soothing Mother Earth voice will somehow hypnotize your now wiggling, babbling little creature back to sleep, but your hum just makes *you* want to doze off...and you can't. Ay, those nights! You, desperately hoping against hope that you're mistaken about the spike in energy your baby is exhibiting. Where did this come from? Why *now*?, your mind yells. How can you be so cute and so exhausting at the same time? Lucky baby.

Hunger you can deal with-whip out a breast, or a bottle, and done. But sometimes, that's not all your baby wants (i.e., that's not all that's going to happen). Be ready for some exhausting, darling, out-of-the-blue play at out-of-the-blue times! (See why naps are vital?) You also know you're in for it when you're feeding him in the wee hours, and he's staring straight into your eyes, *wide awake*...You know then that you are in for a nocturnal tumble with your baby. Marvelous, but maddening...

Her twenty-first week
3 falls, crawling, and a tooth
What a busy gal

I believe it is a misnomer to say that babies have it easy. People will look at a little one being carried in a sling, or being fed by mom, and joke, "Ah, the easy life." In fact, being a baby is hard work! Your nervous system isn't totally developed yet, you are dependent on another person to keep you fed and clean, and for responding to your every discomfort. And your only way to signal is to cry!

You can't even talk yet, everyone is towering above you, and excuse me but what is that car seat *thing* they keep strapping you in and out of while whizzing around town, when all you want to do is be in loving, warm arms like any normal primate? You're trying to sit up, and crawl, but you keep falling. Grrrr! Your messy diapers are getting disgusting even to *you*, your mouth hurts because these hard, sharp things are replacing your squishy soft gums. Everyone else is walking around above you, and you're stuck on the floor!...And did I mention that awful *car seat* thing?...The injustice of it!

Salty streaks
Left on her cheeks by
A good cry

*Teething is
less about teeth than
Saliva*

When your baby starts teething you'll realize why you got 20 bibs at your baby shower. They slobber non-stop! You'll find yourself packing gobs of clean burp cloths and bibs-and a plastic bag to put dirty ones in when you're on the road.

Teething is definitely a messy business. In fact, you may discover his tooth by feeling it even before you see it. With all that slobber in there, it's hard to see. You can feel for teeth by running your finger lightly over his gums. When he's "cut his tooth" you'll feel a sharp part on his gums. Exciting! Now soak up some slobber, take a look and you'll be able to see it-and photograph it of course!

You should start to take care of his teeth once a few have come in. "Brushing" them with your finger and a gauze pad is the simplest way, or you can buy an infant finger brush that looks like a rubber thimble. Cotton probably tastes better to them, though. Some babies have a tougher time with teething. Baby Tylenol, or a dab of good ol' fashion whisky on an emerging tooth, can numb the pain.

Get used to being in his mouth, too. It'll be another seven years until he is completely self-sufficient at brushing his teeth.

An embrace
Quiets her fears and
Dries our tears

The best advice I ever got about calming my daughter was from another mom who told me that "For the first year, just *hold* your baby." All the drama that your baby goes through, and puts you through, will both be cured and calmed by your embrace, your closeness.

Babies are totally vulnerable and they know it. They sense it, and they need to sense that *you* therefore are not only close, but also in charge. If you are panicked that she'll cry again or are distracted while trying to calm her, she'll sense it. Hence, we must learn the ability to "insta-meditate"! (Thank you, Alma!)

To calm my baby, I would hold her firmly against me and do some yoga-style breaths, breathing in deeply, and breathing out slowly from the back of my throat. (It makes sort of a Darth Vaderish sound.) Of course, unintended lessons can come from this…One time after a screaming meltdown of my daughter's, I was calming her down with these yoga breaths, feeling like the Buddha Mama incarnate. She got absolutely still and quiet and I'm thinking *man*, am I good at this mom stuff. I have got it *down*…When suddenly she starts mimicking my breathing, in and out really loudly, then looks at me with a grin…She wasn't putty in my arms after all, she was mocking me–and at 6 months! Grrrr….

Super smiles
After the torrent
Bring relief

Abandoned!
Panicked! Where's my Mom?!
Keep screaming!

It's called "separation anxiety", and not all babies get it. Alma suffered her first bout at 5 months, but it can start a few months later. They are like panic attacks, and they are pitiful and scary. If your baby was never colicky in the early months, but now suffers from separation anxiety, it may be your first bout of what frightening hysteria looks like in your baby (and feels like in your chest).

Different than colic, though, it usually calms immediately when she sees you again. That's how you know it was separation anxiety. You can respond with a kind of "get over it" attitude, as some sociopathic baby-rearing books suggest. Or you can respond in a non-warped, human way and pick her up and hold her tight.

A good way to help your baby get over separation anxiety is to practice saying "goodbye". It's a good socialization skill to teach her anyway. Practice waving goodbye, leaving her sight for a few moments, then reappearing with a big, happy "Hello!" (This is like an early version of peek-a-boo, a universally popular game in the toddler years.)

This kind of panic attack can happen during nighttime sleep, too. They are called "night terrors". Fun, huh? Again, love and closeness to you, and hearing your soothing voice are the answers. There is no way around these attacks, but *through* them. Hang on.

Night Terrors
Require warm arms and
Soft rocking

Hands slapping
Across the tile floor
Stomping crawl

Boy, babies like to show off-loudly! When they become verbal, they babble non-stop to hear their own voices. When they start to eat on their own, their tray becomes a veritable drum set, and when they start crawling, watch out world! Here comes your lil' stompin' Dino!

Babies usually start crawling between 6 and 9 months. The more tummy and floor time early on, the better practice and upper arm strength they will have. You can help by propping him up at times in a semi-crawling position. Don't worry, if he doesn't want it, he'll let you know! Tuck his knees underneath himself, and see if he can push his front up with his arms. He'll know what to do. What an empowering feeling it must be to first become mobile! Go, baby, go!

Soon he'll be "pulling up" (and pulling *down*-careful!) on furniture, and "cruising", using that same furniture to help him walk around the room. Then he'll venture off from the furniture to stand, and take those first steps. Thrilling, for both of you, and a total crack-up!

Arms outstretched
Franken-Baby takes
her first steps

Casu'l leg
Hung out stroller's side.
Mom's drivin'

The pre-verbal stage of a baby's first year is so cute because they are leaving babydom, and starting to act like little non-talking people sometimes. Their mannerisms and imitation of adults are silently developing-and are hilarious. If you've had bad habits until now, Mom, it's time to change them, or to make sure your baby doesn't see or hear them! They are at a *major* mimicking stage.

Now a bit about strollers...I like to keep it simple when it comes to a stroller. Less is more. Less is lighter, too. Something between a flimsy "umbrella" stroller and a turbo-style contraption seems best. I bought one that I could flip and close with one hand. It had a sunshade, a bottom basket, 2 cup holders, reclined and weighed about 6 pounds. Perfect! I took my daughter traveling in the hot, sunny Caribbean in that stroller. With an extra sheet packed below to make a shade tent for her to nap, we could be out all day with our few supplies in tow.

The point is babies need mobility, not mobile homes when they're out with you. Keeping your needs and your stroller simple will make your outings actually *less* stressful. If you think you need the Suburban of Strollers each time you go out, you are less likely to *make* it out, seeing it as too much hassle.

Another funny gesture your "cruising", and maybe now walking (!) baby will start making is pointing to everything in sight! Becoming more upright frees their hands up to point, point, point! (and grab dangerous objects, beware!).

So talk, describe, label their world as your little philosopher points and expounds on it all! Wondrous.

To Point or
not To Point, there is
no question

Cheerios
Have saved this mom's butt
more than once

Yes, I admit it. I was a diehard Cheerio-packer. Ever since I discovered that my daughter loved and could almost always be pacified when need be by the lil' round oat nugget, it became another diaper bag essential. Cheerios, I found, could be substituted in a pinch for her rice cereal, used to distract her from too long of a car ride, and used to buy me time if dinner was going to be late.

Restlessness however, whether in a baby or an adult, is not hunger. If your hands and mind are relatively free, Mom, distract her as much as possible in ways other than food. As someone who has had a lifelong love affair with food, I was aware of the dangers of using it as too much of a "problem solver/boredom reliever" for my baby.

Snack time for the most part was at scheduled intervals, seated, nutritious and with a "purpose". But also take time to just snack and enjoy each other. Have fun with healthy food. I can still visualize where my daughter and I were at this precious blueberry moment, when this poem came to me:

Blueberries
in the small kitchen
With giggles

A flower
And you were made, my
Dear Alma

All moms will wax on lovingly or horrifically about the birth story, but kids will eventually want to know, literally, how they were made. Of course I don't mean you should go into the graphics! But babies will eventually grow into children who will be delighted by their origins. They will be comforted in knowing how much they were wanted and anticipated, even if they were unexpected, and what a joy it was for you to await them.

Whatever your story, conventional or not, don't forget it or bury it, or un-mention it. Your angel's circle of life began with it. Keep telling the stories. Keep the miracle of your love alive for them.

Piles of toys
hold less allure than
Just a few

When it comes to keeping your increasingly active baby entertained later in the year, you might be inclined to dump all his toys out in a big pile, or keep a huge basket full of toys available for him. You might think that unlimited options = longer play, but the opposite ends up being true. Babies get frustrated with too many toy options (and to be honest, aren't we adults overstimulated by all our choices, too?).

It's best to rotate your baby's toys. Take a few out at a time, a couple of soft books and animals, a rattle or two. That's enough for a play session. Rotating his toys keeps 9/10ths of them out of sight at any given time, so as you "rotate" them back into his play, they seem new and interesting again.

Also, try to get in the habit now of not spending a fortune on too many glitzy, loud, battery-devouring, toxin-producing toys shipped brand new from across the ocean to your door…Whew! *Not* sustainable, folks! Check out that great American institution-the Garage Sale-for great bargains. Take that stroller and get to know your neighborhood as you search for hidden treasures for your baby. You'll get to know your neighbors, where the best flower patches are to pick, the nicest dogs and kitties to pet, and you'll need to pack all of $5 to make an entire morning of it! Time, and money, well spent.

And if you're like most of us and have to go back to "work" (as if raising a baby wasn't work), you are racking your brain trying to figure out how to spend more time at home. Start thinking of your *money* as the time away from your baby that it takes to *earn* that money. That is actually a correct equation. Don't waste money, so that you can have more *time*. Look up the group "Planned Simplicity". It's a pioneering organization in the time/money equation, and is now a growing movement in America.

Think sustainability and you will make the right choices. Luckily, conserving the environment and conserving our paychecks are mutually reinforcing: The less #@!%# we buy, the less resources we use and the more money (i.e. time) we save to spend it where we really want to, and should: with our angels.

It's true what they say, too, that often a child's favorite part of a new toy is the box. Get creative. Fill a box with clothes and watch her try to dress herself from it, or play peek-a-boo with it, or fill it with her toys. Let's look around our houses for fun things to play with. At bath time, for instance, bring out the kitchen funnels, colanders, and measuring cups to entertain her toward the end of that first year. Remember those? They are free, and multi-purpose.

> *Tupperware*
> *is a "poor baby's"*
> *favorite toy*

Mom's Courage
in these intense times
is stretched thin

Life will happen while you raise your baby. Housing, jobs, family problems, wars, and the general painful side of humanity. There are many issues pulling you in all directions. You and your baby are your foundation, your rudder. Stay close and the answers will come. Taking action on what makes you afraid or angry will empower you.

It's a funny thing about being a new mom. You are at once so tender, yet have potentially ferocious power now that you have something so precious to protect. So warmongers, beware a wave of Mama Righteousness! Change them, one at a time, with the truth of what you are doing, the love you are feeling for your baby. *Your* day is spent in the most human and productive of ways. Keep remembering that, and look always to which forces are supporting you and your baby, and the world's babies.

If you need to get assistance from the government to care for your baby for a while, go ahead! And don't feel guilty about it. The way I see it, you've paid into it, now you need it. So find money and use it, be with your baby and raise a peacemaker, a strong community member. It's a good investment and any government in its right mind should thank you. Ours will not, so be resourceful, and feel the support and common cause of billions of moms around the world.

We are doing beautiful work, at times against great odds. We are all struggling in our ways, wanting a sane, more safe, more just world. How to change it, yet live *in* it in these intense times is a dilemma.

She and I
Against the world
Yet among it

Oh, those eyes!
challenging me at
just One Year...

Did you know that one of your baby's favorite words next year will be "No"?...Get ready, Mom!

CPSIA information can be obtained at www.ICGtesting.com
Printed in the USA
LVOW042224230512

283031LV00001B/10/P